EDGE OF MEDICINE

MEDICAL
INVENTION
BREAKTHROUGHS

HEATHER E. SCHWARTZ

MAYO CLINIC PRESS KIDS

To Philip, Jaz, and Griffin

MAYO CLINIC PRESS KIDS | An imprint of Mayo Clinic Press
200 First St. SW
Rochester, MN 55905
mcpress.mayoclinic.org
To stay informed about Mayo Clinic Press, please subscribe to our free e-newsletter at mcpress.mayoclinic.org or follow us on social media.

The medical information in this book is true and complete to the best of our knowledge. This book is intended as an informative guide for those wishing to learn more about health issues. It is not intended to replace, countermand or conflict with advice given to you by your own physician. The ultimate decision concerning your care should be made between you and your doctor. Information in this book is offered with no guarantees. The author and publisher disclaim all liability in connection with the use of this book. The views expressed are the author's personal views, and do not necessarily reflect the policy or position of Mayo Clinic.

For bulk sales to employers, member groups and health-related companies, contact Mayo Clinic at SpecialSalesMayoBooks@mayo.edu.

Proceeds from the sale of every book benefit important medical research and education at Mayo Clinic.

ISBN: 978-1-945564-90-1 (paperback) | 978-1-945564-89-5 (library) | 978-1-945564-91-8 (ebook) | 979-8-88770-084-7 (multiuser PDF) | 979-8-88770-083-0 (multiuser ePub)

Library of Congress Control Number: 2022942579
Library of Congress Cataloging-in-Publication Data is available upon request.

TABLE OF CONTENTS

SCIENTISTS INVENT
SOLUTIONS

In 1928, Scottish doctor Alexander Fleming took a vacation. He left **culture plates** of bacteria uncovered in his lab. When Fleming returned, he found a **fungus** had grown on one of the plates. Instead of throwing the bacteria away, Fleming observed it. And he made a discovery!

Fleming noticed that wherever the fungus had grown, there was no longer bacteria. The fungus was acting as a treatment, killing the bacteria. Fleming had discovered penicillin!

Experiments proved the fungus penicillin could treat many diseases. It could also kill **infections**. Scientists made several types of penicillin antibiotics. The fungus became the first mass-produced antibiotic.

Throughout history, problems have inspired scientists to make medical inventions. When a solution doesn't exist, they create it. These inventions save and improve people's lives and create a cutting-edge future in medicine.

Alexander Fleming examines a penicillin mold in 1943. Fleming became famous for his discovery and came to be known as a global ambassador for medicine and science.

DISCOVERING X-RAYS
BY ACCIDENT

One day in 1895, German scientist Wilhelm Röntgen was testing cathode rays. A cathode is a metallic part from which electrons stream out of an electrical device. These streams are called rays. They give off **ultraviolet radiation**. Röntgen wanted to know more about the rays.

Röntgen used thick black paper and a **fluorescent** screen to explore whether the rays could pass through glass. What he learned surprised him. A bright green light passed through the black paper and onto the screen! The light ray was a form Röntgen had never seen. He had no idea what these rays were. So he named them "X" rays and kept experimenting.

The scientist found X-rays could pass through nearly anything to produce shadowy images—even through human **tissue**! This created images of bones inside the body. Röntgen shared his findings with doctors, who were amazed by the technology and began using it by the next year.

X-rays allowed doctors to see patients' **internal** problems. This allowed doctors to provide better treatments, and in many cases, even spare patients from **surgery**! X-rays became standard in medical care. Modern doctors use them to diagnose illness, find swallowed objects, and much more.

Wilhelm Röntgen's X-ray technology being used to produce an image of the hand

INVENTION DIAGNOSES
HEART DISORDERS

B y 1900, scientists had learned that the heart gives off electrical activity. In the early 1900s, Dutch doctor Willem Einthoven invented a machine that showed the activity on paper. The machine was a string galvanometer. It had **electromagnets** and strings covered in silver, which conducts electricity.

The string galvanometer weighed 600 pounds (272 kg) and took five people to operate! Patients had to sit with their limbs in buckets of salt water, which conducted electricity. Then the string galvanometer **monitored** the patient's heart.

The machine drew the heart's electrical **impulses** as wavy lines on paper. Different heart conditions made different line patterns. This helped doctors diagnose heart conditions.

The string galvanometer was an early version of the **electrocardiograph** machine (ECG). In an ECG, sticky patches called **electrodes** take the place of buckets of salt water. The electrodes are attached to a patient's chest and to a monitor using wires.

Willem Einthoven beside his string galvanometer

ACCELERATES TREATMENT

The winter of 1905 was a cold one in Minnesota. And the freezing temperatures led to a medical discovery. In January, doctor Louis B. Wilson arrived in the state to help Mayo Clinic doctors improve the way they diagnosed **cancer**.

Mayo's current process began with doctors surgically removing tissue samples. They tested the samples and waited days for results. If the results showed cancer, the doctors did a second surgery to remove it. But they wanted to diagnose and remove cancer in one surgery. Wilson had an idea.

Wilson put a tissue sample on a hospital window ledge, where it froze in the cold. Then, he dyed and sliced the frozen tissue so he could view it on a slide under a **microscope**. This allowed him to easily see the cells and diagnose whether they contained cancer.

Wilson continued experimenting. After a few months, he had the process down. Instead of days, Wilson could make a diagnosis in less than five minutes! This meant the full test could be completed during the patient's first surgery. If results of the test showed cancer, surgeons could remove it right then. This ended the need for two surgeries.

Louis B. Wilson's technique to diagnose and treat cancer in one surgery became standard in medical care.

PORTABLE
LIFESAVER

Cardiac arrest is when a person's heart stops beating. By the late 1800s, doctors had learned they could apply electrical current directly to the heart to restart it. This process is called defibrillation.

By the 1950s, scientists improved defibrillation. They no longer applied current directly to the heart. Instead, they sent electric shocks to the heart through the person's chest.

For the patient to survive, defibrillation must occur within five minutes of cardiac arrest. At first, defibrillators were only in hospitals. So the process could only happen if the patient was already in the hospital when their heartbeat stopped. Irish doctor Frank Pantridge wanted to change this.

In 1965, Pantridge invented a portable **automated** external defibrillator (AED). It was powered by car and so could be operated in an ambulance.

Today, there are battery-powered AEDs that are kept in many public spaces. These include grocery stores, airports,

AED electrodes are attached to a mannequin for demonstration. The electrodes gather information about the heart's rhythm. If the AED determines the person does not need a shock, the device will not deliver one.

and even schools. Police officers and other emergency workers are trained to use the devices. AEDs save about 1,700 lives in the United States each year.

PRIVATE
PREGNANCY TEST

When a person needs to find out if they are pregnant, they may want to do it in private. But in the 1960s, the only way to confirm pregnancy was by visiting a doctor's office or waiting for body changes. Both methods could delay important **prenatal** care. Margaret Crane changed this.

Crane was a graphic designer. In 1967, she worked for **pharmaceutical** company Organon. In Organon's labs, she saw pregnancy tests being processed. Patients' urine was held in test tubes. The urine was mixed with **reagents**. A chemical reaction revealed whether the patient was pregnant.

The test setup looked simple to Crane—simple enough she felt patients could do it themselves! Crane decided to design a do-it-yourself kit. She made a **prototype** of parts using materials she had at home. Crane wasn't able to create the chemical parts of the test. But Organon could. Crane sold her prototype to the company. Organon began creating and selling the devices. Crane had invented the first home pregnancy test!

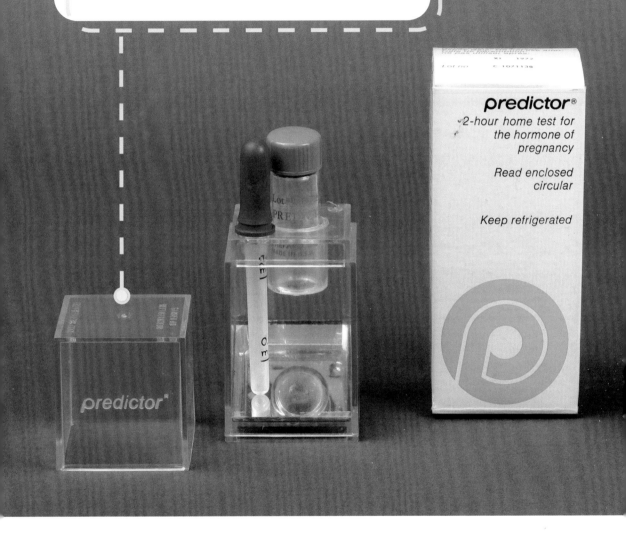

Margaret Crane's creation was sold under the name Predictor. Each box contained all items a person needed to test for pregnancy at home.

A majority of modern pregnancies are now detected using a home test. People can learn the life-changing news of a pregnancy in private. And they can start getting prenatal care right away.

JENNIFER L. FANG, MD

MAYO CLINIC

Q: What do you like best about treating newborn babies?

A: I like helping babies immediately after birth as they make one of the biggest transitions in life. I enjoy leading a team that cares for very sick, vulnerable babies and helps them get well. Most of all, I love seeing our patients leave the neonatal intensive care unit (NICU), go home with their families, and grow up into smiling, active children.

Q: What are the most exciting medical inventions being developed today?

A: The neonatal ICU can be a scary place for caregivers

and families. Their baby is in a special bed, with many technologies attached. It's exciting that people are inventing devices to measure vital signs and blood values without invasive lines or procedures. Health care teams are also inventing ways for families to stay connected to their newborn even when they can't be with their baby in the hospital. There are technologies that allow families to connect to a secure video of their newborn so they can view their baby at any time from any place that has an internet connection.

Q: How can telemedicine improve medical care?

A: Telemedicine can increase patients' access to health care that would otherwise be really hard to get. For example, we have been using telemedicine to have our neonatologists (doctors with special training to care for very sick babies) provide video consults when a very sick baby is born in a small hospital that doesn't have specialists. Our telemedicine consults improve the babies' care by making sure their temperature, blood sugar, and breathing are monitored appropriately. Telemedicine consults can also make it possible for babies to stay in the hospital with their mothers instead of needing to come by ambulance or helicopter to a faraway neonatal ICU.

FAST
ANTHRAX TEST

On September 11, 2001, **terrorists** attacked several US buildings. Many people were killed. In the months following, it appeared the attack wasn't over.

Someone laced letters with the bacteria *Bacillus anthracis* and mailed them to US media outlets and congressional offices. *Bacillus anthracis* causes the deadly disease anthrax. Anthrax contracted from the letters killed five people and made 22 more sick. It was the worst biological attack the country had experienced.

Scientists sought a way to save people exposed to any more poisoned letters. At the time, test results for anthrax took up to three days to process. People exposed could die in that time.

Mayo Clinic scientists joined with Roche Diagnostics to create a faster test. The test examined a person's **DNA** for

A microbiologist tests for *Bacillus anthracis*, the bacteria that causes anthrax, in 2001. The bacteria forms spores. Anthrax forms if people breathe in, eat, or expose open wounds to these spores.

traces of the bacteria that causes anthrax. Former anthrax tests had to be sent to a highly specialized lab for processing. Mayo's test could diagnose anthrax in less than one hour.

Mayo's test was mass produced so medical centers across the country would have it on hand. And during the public scare about anthrax, Mayo and Roche Diagnostics gave medical centers and laboratories across the United States test kits for free. If more poisoned letters were sent, people could be tested in minutes and get care that could save their lives.

1 *Bacillus anthracis* spores are inhaled.

2 *Bacillus anthracis* spores enter the lungs and travel to air-containing (alveolar) spaces.

Toxins

Spores

3 Spores are transported through the lymph system to glands that lie between the sternum and the spinal column (mediastinal lymph nodes), where they make deadly toxins.

The process of *Bacillus anthracis* spores being inhaled and causing anthrax to form

CANCER VACCINE
SAVES PATIENTS

In 2009, nearly 200,000 people in the United States were diagnosed with prostate cancer. US doctors Edgar G. Engleman and Reiner Laus felt the widespread cancer needed better treatment. The pair had spent years researching possible new treatments.

Engleman and Laus turned to **vaccines** during their study. The doctors knew vaccines cause the **immune system** to create **proteins** that can fight disease. They wondered if a vaccine could cause a direct attack instead. Engleman and Laus wanted to create a vaccine that would direct the immune system to attack and kill prostate cancer cells.

The doctors succeeded! Engleman and Laus's invention, sipuleucel-T, causes the immune system to attack an **antigen** found in prostate cancer cells. The doctors' vaccine underwent **clinical trials**. In 2010, it became the first government-approved cancer vaccine. Sipuleucel-T is a **unique** vaccine in that it is a treatment, and not a prevention.

Eighty-year-old US patient Bob Svensson receives sipuleucel-T treatment in 2010. The treatment involves collecting patient immune cells, activating them with the vaccine, and returning the cells to the patient's body three days later.

AR SURGERY ASSISTANCE

Suppose you needed spinal surgery. Would you feel confident if your surgeon did the job while wearing a headset? The device might look like a video game accessory. But it's actually cutting-edge technology made to assist with surgery!

US inventor Nissan Elimelech received government approval to create and sell the xvision in 2019. It is a headset vision guidance system. The device uses **augmented reality** (AR) to turn a **scan** of a patient's spine into a 3D image. Surgeons wear the headset during surgery. The device projects the AR image on top of the patient's body. It is almost as though the surgeon is able to operate with X-ray vision!

AR headset guidance systems allow surgeons to look at the AR image and the patient at the same time. Earlier surgical assistance devices required using an extra screen showing the patient's scan. AR guidance systems can improve **accuracy** and lessen the time a surgery takes.

Nissan Elimelech (*center*) presented his idea for xvision (*worn by man on right*) at a technology convention in 2017. The screen behind the inventor shows the xvision wearer's view of an AR image through the device.

BEDSORE
SCANNER

Some patients have a slow recovery after surgery. Many must spend a lot of time lying in bed, which puts pressure on certain areas of the body. This can cause pressure **ulcers** called bedsores to form. They appear on the skin but go deep into tissue. Bedsores can get infected and even cause death.

In the past, health care workers had to see bedsores to diagnose them. It was difficult to find bedsores on patients who couldn't move. And there was no process for spotting the sores before they were visible on the skin—until 2020!

That year, scientists at the University of California, Los Angeles invented the Provizio SEM Scanner. It detects moisture beneath the skin, a sign a bedsore is forming underneath. When the scanner reports moisture in a certain location, nurses can move the patient's body to remove pressure from that spot. This can stop the bedsore in its tracks.

By 2020, 30 US hospitals were using the scanner. Combined, these hospitals' cases of bedsores went down 90 percent.

BEDSORE LOCATIONS AND STAGES

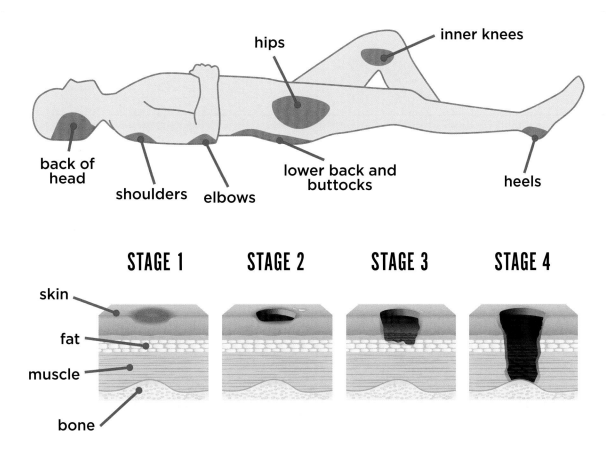

A bedsore scanner, spinal surgery headset, and X-rays are just some amazing medical inventions. Medical teams worldwide are constantly experimenting to create more. The inventions of tomorrow may save millions of lives!

TIMELINE

EARLY 1900s

Willem Einthoven invents the string galvanometer. It shows heart activity as wavy lines on paper, helping doctors diagnose different disorders.

1928

Alexander Fleming discovers penicillin. It becomes the first mass-produced antibiotic, curing many diseases.

1895

Wilhelm Röntgen discovers X-rays, which can be used to diagnose patients without surgery.

1965

Frank Pantridge invents the portable automated external defibrillator. It can restart a person's heart outside medical settings.

1905

Louis B. Wilson develops a frozen section technique to diagnose cancer during surgery.

2010

A prostate cancer vaccine developed by Edgar G. Engleman and Reiner Laus gets government approval.

1967

Margaret Crane invents the physical parts of the first home pregnancy test. It allows people to test for pregnancy at home.

2020

University of California scientists invent a tool to detect bedsores. The device reduces bedsore treatment needs by 90 percent.

2001

Mayo Clinic and Roche Diagnostics develop a fast test for anthrax exposure. The faster results allow for earlier treatment, saving lives.

2019

Nissan Elimelech sells the xvision for spine surgeries. It improves surgical accuracy using an augmented reality headset.

GLOSSARY

accuracy—the degree to which something is free from mistakes or error

antigen—a substance that causes the immune system to create antibodies

augmented reality—technology that puts a computer-generated image on a user's view of the real world

automated—completed with little or no human assistance

cancer—a group of often deadly diseases in which harmful cells spread quickly

clinical trial—a study done to see how efficient and safe a new or emerging treatment is

culture plate—a low, flat-bottomed dish used to grow organisms on a thin layer of nutrient medium

DNA—a molecule in cells that holds genetic information

electrocardiograph—an instrument used to record potential electrical changes during a heartbeat

electrode—a conductor through which electricity leaves or enters

electromagnet—a magnet whose magnetic field is created by electric current

fluorescent—producing light when electricity flows through a tube filled with a type of gas

fungus—one of a group of living things, such as molds and mushrooms, that are neither plants nor animals

immune system—the body's system that fights off disease and infection

impulse—a wave of energy transmitted through tissues, nerve fibers, and muscles that results in activity

infection—the entrance and growth of germs in the body. Being in this state is called being infected.

internal—inside the body

microscope—a device containing a powerful magnifying glass used to see items invisible to the human eye

monitor—to watch or keep track of. An electronic device with a screen used for display is also called a monitor.

pharmaceutical—relating to the preparation, use, or sale of drugs used as medicine

prenatal—before birth

protein—a molecule of amino acids that is essential to body function

prototype—an original type, form, or model

reagent—a substance or mixture for use in chemical analysis or other reactions

scan—an image of a body part, produced using medical technology. A scanner is a device that can produce these images.

surgery—a medical treatment performed on internal body parts. This treatment is performed by a surgeon.

terrorist—a person who uses violence to try and achieve political goals

tissue—a group of like cells that work together in the body to perform a function

ulcer—a painful, sore area inside or outside the body

ultraviolet radiation—a type of energy produced by the sun and some artificial sources

unique—unlike anything else

vaccine—a medication prepared and given, often by injection, to protect a person against a disease

LEARN MORE

How to Be Good at Science, Technology, and Engineering. London: DK Children, 2018.

Mayo Clinic: Contributions to Medicine
https://history.mayoclinic.org/toolkit/contributions-to-medicine.php

National Geographic Kids: Science with Dr. Karl: Extraordinary X-Rays
https://www.natgeokids.com/uk/discover/science/general-science/science-dr-karl-extraordinary-x-rays/

Stoltman, Joan. *Weird Medical Inventions*. New York: Gareth Stevens Publishing, 2018.

INDEX

PHOTO ACKNOWLEDGMENTS

AP Images, pp. 5, 28 (top); Artur Plawgo/iStockphoto, cover (tumor cells); Dave Martin/AP Images, p. 19; Elise Amendola/AP Images, p. 23; Mayo Clinic, pp. 11, 16, 21, 28 (bottom); Mykhailo Pervak/iStockphoto, back cover; National Museum of American History, Behring Center Archives Center, p. 15; Nicolae Malancea/iStockphoto, cover (culture dish); NLM/Science Source, p. 9; ollo/iStockphoto, p. 13; riopatuca/Shutterstock Images, cover (doctor and headset); Science Source, p. 7; solar22/iStockphoto, p. 27 (top, bottom); Steve Jennings/TechCrunch/Flickr, pp. 25, 29; traffic_analyzer/iStockphoto, cover (background); xavierarnau/iStockphoto, cover (child and nurse)